Our Lives as Caterpillars

Craig E. Briggs

illustrated by Anya Latham

ISBN: 1484179293
ISBN-13: 9781484179291

PREFACE

The death of a loved one is a painful and frightening experience. It is difficult at any age to understand and process the powerful emotions and feelings of loss that accompany such an event. This can be especially true for children, who may ask, "Why do the ones we love have to die?" "Why is Grandma no longer here?" "Where did she go?"

Our Lives as Caterpillars provides a framework for adults to discuss with young children the difficult topic of death. It enables parents to acknowledge the sadness and sense of loss that their child is experiencing following the death of a pet, family member, or friend. In addition, it conveys to the child a sense of hope regarding this life-changing event. The book accomplishes this without interjecting or imposing any particular religious belief regarding life after death and, in fact, without using the word *death* at all. The book was written following the death of my wife, Janis Briggs, a beloved spouse, mother, grandmother, public school music teacher, and friend. It tells her story-our story. The inspiration for the book came in part from this quotation, attributed to A.A. Milne, which hung in the waiting room at the natural healing center where Jan received treatment for breast cancer.

> "How does one become a butterfly?" Pooh asked pensively....
> "You must want to fly so badly that you're willing to give up being a caterpillar," Piglet replied.
> "You mean you die?" asked Pooh.
> "Yes and no," he answered. "What looks like you will die, but what's Really you will live on."

As Jan's cancer progressed and in the days prior to her death, I often used the metaphor of caterpillars becoming butterflies when we would talk about her impending departure. I would reassure her that we were all caterpillars becoming butterflies, and that she would be the one to undergo this metamorphosis first. We were both comforted by our belief that our love for each other would overcome death and that, someday, I would join her as a butterfly.

This book is dedicated to Jan. She lives on. I hope that the book will bring some measure of hope and comfort to anyone experiencing the death of a loved one.

Craig Briggs April 2013

In a small village next to a big lake in the mountains, there lived many caterpillars. The lake was called Lake George, and the mountains were called the Adirondacks.

In the village, there was a school for young caterpillars.

On the first day of school, in the year 1963,
two new caterpillars came to the school to teach.
The new teachers' names were Jan and Craig.

Jan loved music, so she taught music.
Craig loved history, so he taught history.
Before long, they fell deeply in love.

Jan and Craig got married and moved to a new village called Canterbury, in a land called New Hampshire.

Soon Jan and Craig had four baby caterpillars,
and they became a family. They named their children
Amy, Jennifer, John, and Sarah.

The family of six caterpillars lived happily on a farm called the Good Earth Farm. Jan taught them many things, like how to grow their own food and how to love music.

7

But most of all, Jan taught them how to love each other
and to love all caterpillars. The family was very happy,
and their love for each other grew and grew and grew.

One day, Jan felt very strange.
She and Craig went to visit the doctor.

The doctor said, "You are changing
and will not be a caterpillar much longer."
"But I love being a caterpillar!" Jan said.
"Why can't I be a caterpillar forever?"

The doctor replied, "I don't know exactly why,
but caterpillars are living things, and nothing
that is living stays the same forever."

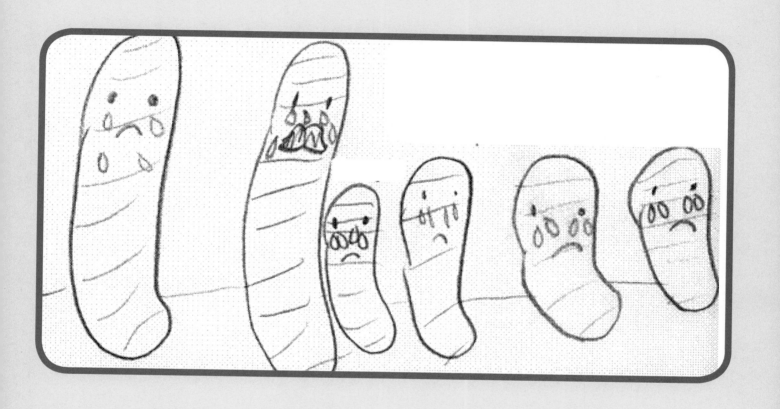

Jan and Craig were very sad. Their children were very sad.
Their friends were very sad. It was a sad time for all
of the caterpillars who knew and loved Jan.

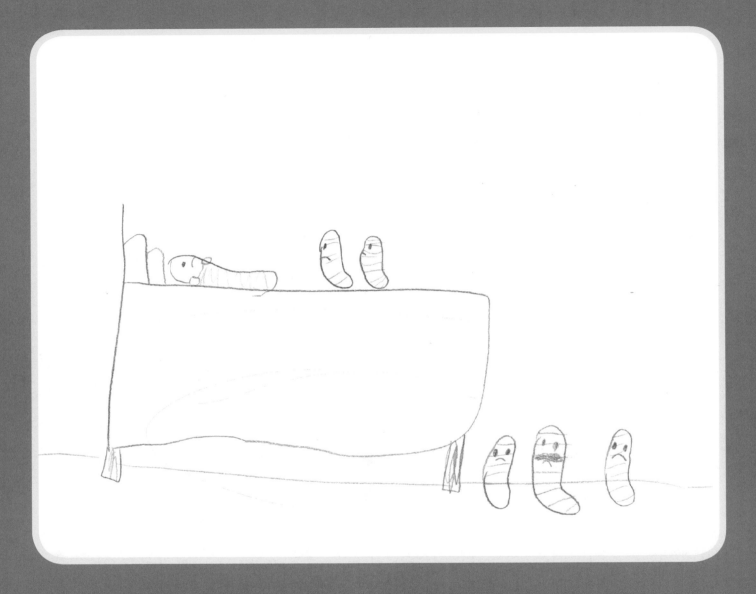

One night, Jan felt very sick and could not get out of bed.
The family knew that it was the time when Jan would
stop being a caterpillar. They were all afraid.

When the time came for Jan to stop being a caterpillar, something amazing happened that made the family happy, especially Jan. She stopped feeling sick, and even better than that, she became more beautiful than she had been as a caterpillar. And Jan was a very beautiful caterpillar!

Jan no longer looked like a caterpillar. She had beautifully colored wings, and best of all, she could fly! She was a beautiful butterfly, free to go everywhere, and to be with other beautiful butterflies in a very beautiful land of flowers and sunshine.

The caterpillars were happy for Jan but sad for themselves. They were still dull-looking caterpillars with no wings. They couldn't fly. They couldn't go with Jan to that beautiful place.

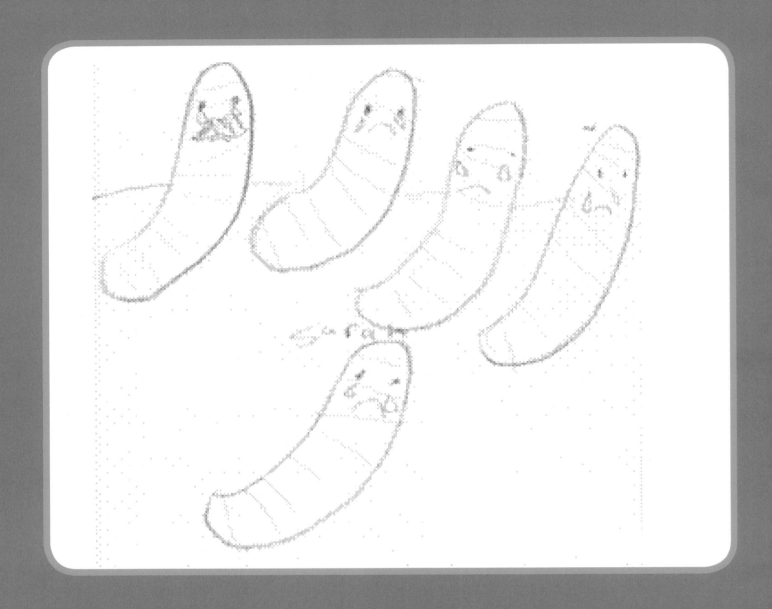

Jan's family was sadder than they could ever remember being.
What will we do without her? they wondered.

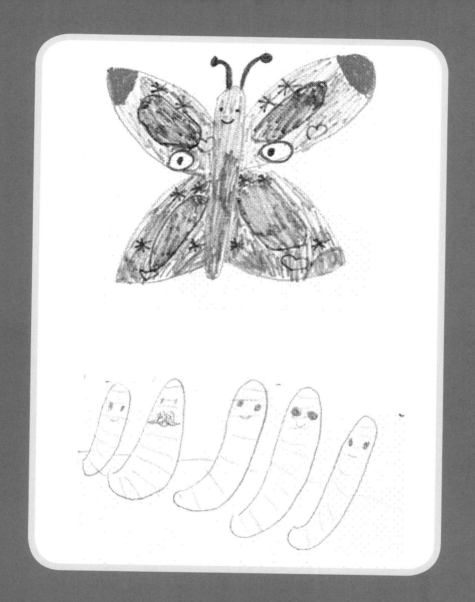

Then one day, soon after Jan had become a butterfly, they felt the breeze from her wings as she fluttered high above them. They could not see her, but they knew it was Jan.

"Love," they heard her say. "It's all about love! I am in a place of pure love, and someday you will be here, too. So don't be sad, be happy and love one another. I will wait for you here."